CULTURE IN ACTION

Ballroom Dancing

Deborah Underwood

Chicago, Illinois

www.heinemannraintree.com
Visit our website to find out more information about Heinemann-Raintree books.

To order:
☎ Phone 888-454-2279
🖥 Visit www.heinemannraintree.com to browse our catalog and order online.

©2010 Raintree
an imprint of Capstone Global Library, LLC
Chicago, Illinois

Edited by Louise Galpine, Abby Colich, and Laura J. Hensley
Designed by Kimberly Miracle and Betsy Wernert
Original illustrations © Capstone Global Library Ltd.
Illustrated by kja-artists.com
Picture research by Hannah Taylor
Production by Alison Parsons
Originated by Dot Gradations Ltd.
Printed and Bound in the United States
by Corporate Graphics

13 12 11 10 09
10 9 8 7 6 5 4 3 2 1

Library of Congress Cataloging-in-Publication Data

Underwood, Deborah.
  Ballroom dancing / Deborah Underwood. -- 1st ed.
     p. cm. -- (Culture in action)
  Includes bibliographical references and index.
  ISBN 978-1-4109-3398-0 (hc) -- ISBN 978-1-4109-3415-4 (pb)
  1. Ballroom dancing--Juvenile literature. I. Title.
  GV1751.U53 2008
  793.3'3--dc22
                              2008053059

Acknowledgments

The author and publishers are grateful to the following for permission to reproduce copyright material: Alamy pp. **5** (© ilian stage), **8** (© Geoff A. Howard); Corbis pp. **6** (Fancy/ Veer), **10** & **13** (Bettmann), **22** (Reuters/Will Burgess), **24** (Chris Faytok); Getty Images pp. **12** (Alexander Hassenstein), **14** (Angelo Cavalli), **16** (NBC Television), **18** (Graphic House), **21** (Clive Rose), **23** (Sergio Dionisio), **27** (AFP Photo/Viktor Drachev); Photolibrary pp. **7** (Digital Vision), **20** (Nonstock/ Echos), **26** (Ryan Mcvay); Photoshot p. **4** (WpN); Rex Features pp. **17** & **25** (Sipa Press).

Icon and banner images supplied by Shutterstock: © Alexander Lukin, © ornitopter, © Colorlife, and © David S. Rose.

Cover photograph of a ballroom dancing couple reproduced with permission of Getty/PM Images.

We would like to thank Nancy Harris, Jackie Murphy, and Sarah Whatley for their invaluable help in the preparation of this book.

Contents

Some words are printed in bold, **like this**. You can find out what they mean by looking in the glossary on page 30.

What Is Ballroom Dancing?

In a gym, a group of 10-year-olds learns a dance called the **waltz**. During a competition, skilled dancers in fancy costumes glide across the floor. In a senior center, men and women swirl around the room to music playing from a CD player. All these people are enjoying ballroom dancing.

Ballroom dancing is a kind of dancing done in pairs. Each pair has a leader (usually a man). It also has a follower (usually a woman).

The leader and the follower communicate—but not by talking. They communicate by using their bodies. The leader moves in a way that tells the follower which step is next. The follower also communicates. She may notice that she and her partner are too close to other dancers. If she does, she can gently pull her partner forward. This tells him that there is someone behind him.

People of all ages enjoy ballroom dancing.

Different dances

There are many different ballroom dances. They are danced to different kinds of music. Each one has different steps and **rhythms** (patterns of beats). Some dances are slow and flowing. Others are fast and bouncy. In some dances, the partners hold each other all the time. In others, they may dance without touching for a while.

People enjoy ballroom dancing for many reasons. Some people like to dance in competitions. Others like the fact that ballroom dancing is good exercise. But mostly people like ballroom dancing because it is fun!

Young dancers can compete in special ballroom dancing contests for students.

Ballroom Basics

There are two main styles of ballroom dancing: International style and American style. International style is the most common of the two, but both styles are popular in the United States.

At an International-style dance contest, there are 10 different dances. The dances can be divided into two groups. One group is called **International Standard**. The other is known as **International Latin**.

Listed below are the International Standard and International Latin dances.

INTERNATIONAL STANDARD
waltz
fox-trot
tango
quickstep
Viennese waltz

INTERNATIONAL LATIN
cha-cha
rumba
samba
paso doble
jive

American-style dancing

American Smooth dances include the **waltz**, the **tango**, the **fox-trot**, and the **Viennese waltz**. They have the same names as some International Standard dances. But the American dances are done differently. For example, dancers may dance in **open position** (see photo). The American **Rhythm** group includes the **cha-cha** and **rumba**. So does the International Latin group. It also includes three other dances: the **bolero**, the **mambo**, and the East Coast **swing**.

In open positions, ballroom dancers may hold hands. They do not necessarily face each other.

These dancers are standing in closed position. The man's right hand is on the woman's back. The woman's left hand is on the man's shoulder. Their other hands are clasped together.

There are five International Standard dances (see box on page 6). In most of these, the dancers keep their upper bodies still. Standard dances are done in **closed position**. This means the partners hold each other and face each other.

There are also five International Latin dances (see box on page 6). For these, the dancers do not need to stay in closed position. Some of these dances, such as the **samba** and the **jive**, are fast and bouncy.

These dancers are dancing a progressive dance.

Moving to the music

In some dances, the couple moves around the ballroom. These are called **progressive dances**. Couples move along what is called the **line of dance**, an imaginary counterclockwise circle on the dance floor. All the couples move in the same direction. This helps to stop couples from crashing into one another. All International Standard dances are progressive. Two International Latin dances, the samba and the **paso doble**, are progressive.

The rumba, cha-cha, and jive are **spot dances**. During a spot dance, the dancers stay in the same area of the dance floor. This makes spot dances easier to dance in a crowded ballroom than progressive dances.

Feel the waltz rhythm!

Waltz music is written in **triple meter**. This means the beats in the music come in groups of three. This is its rhythm.

Steps to follow:

1. Stand up and count out loud: "One-two-three, one-two-three, one-two-three, one-two-three." Keep your counting of the numbers steady.

2. Now do the same thing, but stress the ones: "ONE-two-three, ONE-two-three, ONE-two-three, ONE-two-three."

3. As you say "ONE," bend your knees.

4. As you say "two-three," rise up again.

5. Now try walking in waltz rhythm. Take one step for each count. To really get the waltz feeling, sink down on "ONE," then rise up on your toes for "two-three" as you walk.

6. Ask an adult to put on some waltz music, such as "The Rainbow Connection" or "Moon River." Try to walk with the beat. The waltz is a graceful dance. Imagine yourself floating around a ballroom in fancy clothes!

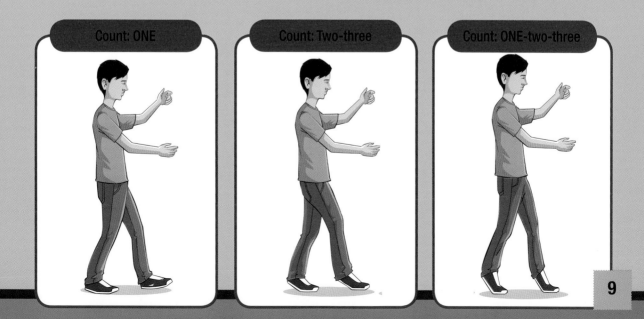

Count: ONE

Count: Two-three

Count: ONE-two-three

Dances of the Past

Many ballroom dances began less than 100 years ago, but people have danced since ancient times. In 1588 a French priest wrote a book describing over 40 social dances of the time, including the pavane and the allemande. These are some of the earliest ballroom dances.

In the 1600s, the **minuet** was a popular dance in France and England. The minuet is a slow, elegant dance. The dancers take small steps and turn their toes outward.

The minuet was a popular dance in ballrooms from about 1650 until 1750.

quickstep
England

waltz
Germany/Austria

EUROPE

Viennese waltz
Germany/Austria

NORTH
AMERICA

Atlantic Ocean

cha-cha
Cuba

rumba
Cuba

paso doble
Spain

jive
United States

fox-trot
United States

SOUTH
AMERICA

Pacific Ocean

samba
Brazil

Indian Ocean

tango
Argentina

N
W E
S

This map shows where some of today's ballroom dances began.

Dances from around the world

Today's ballroom dances draw from many countries. The **samba** comes from Brazil. The **tango** is from Argentina. Some dances are based on **folk dances** (dances of a nation's common people). The **Viennese waltz** is based on a German and Austrian folk dance called the ländler.

Some people did not welcome new dances. Many people were angry when the **waltz** came to England. They believed it was not proper for men and women to dance so close to each other. In 1816 an article about waltzing appeared in a London newspaper. It warned parents not to let their daughters do the waltz! But the waltz became popular anyway.

Dancing and music

An important part of any dance is the music. Today, people can hear music whenever they want. But in the 1800s, there were no radios, CD players, or MP3 players. People could only dance if musicians played for them. At a party, one person might play a piano so others could dance, or the host might hire musicians to play.

Standard Dances

International Standard dances include the **Viennese waltz**, the **waltz**, the **tango**, the **fox-trot**, and the **quickstep**. These are all **progressive dances**. All are danced in **closed position**. Most are danced to music from Europe or the United States.

Viennese waltz

The word *waltz* comes from the German word meaning "turn." During the Viennese waltz, couples spin as they move around the dance floor. The Viennese waltz is danced to music with a **triple meter**.

The Viennese waltz came to England in 1812. Many **composers** (people who write music) enjoyed creating music for it. Austrian composers Johann Strauss and Josef Lanner wrote a lot of Viennese waltz music. Their music helped make the Viennese waltz popular.

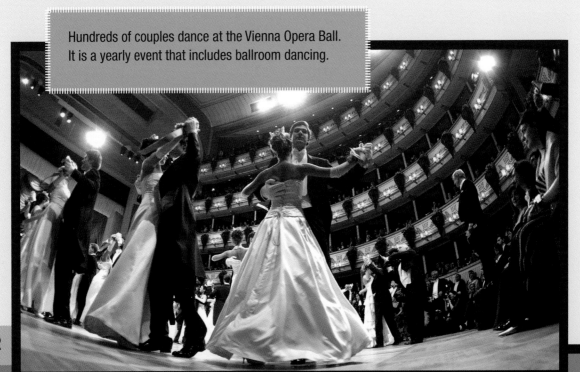

Hundreds of couples dance at the Vienna Opera Ball. It is a yearly event that includes ballroom dancing.

Waltz

Over time, some people began to dance the waltz in a different way. In the United States, people started waltzing more slowly. This dance was called the slow waltz, or the **Boston**. The Boston had fewer spins than the Viennese waltz. Its steps were longer and smoother. In some places, it became more popular than the Viennese waltz.

Today's waltz is related to the Boston. It is an elegant dance with flowing moves. Like the Viennese waltz, it is danced to music with a triple meter.

Fred Astaire and Ginger Rogers made movies filled with dancing.

Astaire and Rogers

U.S. actors and dancers Fred Astaire and Ginger Rogers appeared together in 10 movie musicals. They often mixed ballroom dances with other dance styles, such as tap dance. In one movie they even danced on roller skates! Because of these movies, many people became interested in ballroom dancing.

Tango

The tango began in Argentina. It became popular in France around 1907. Soon after, the tango swept England. A dancer named Maurice Mouvet first performed the tango in New York City in 1910.

Tango dancers press their bodies close together. Quick head movements are often part of this dance.

Theatrical poses are part of the tango.

Fox-trot

The fox-trot began in New York City around 1914. It may have been named after Harry Fox, a U.S. actor who did the dance onstage. Or it may have been named after the animal the fox. "Animal" dances, such as the bunny hug and the turkey trot, were popular at that time. The fox-trot quickly spread to England.

The fox-trot is made up of smooth, gliding movements. It mixes slow walks with fast, trotting steps.

Quickstep

A new dance was introduced at a dance contest in England in 1927. It mixed a fast fox-trot with the Charleston, another popular dance. Over time this dance became known as the quickstep.

The quickstep uses faster music than the fox-trot. It looks smooth, even though it has a lot of hops, runs, and turns.

Learn the box step

The box step can be part of dances such as the waltz and the **rumba**.

Steps to follow:

1. Trace each of your feet onto a separate sheet of paper three times.

2. Color the left feet one color. Number them 1, 3, and 5.

3. Color the right feet another color. Number them 2, 4, and 6.

4. Cut out the feet, then set them up as shown in the picture below.

5. Start by standing on 5 and 6.

6. Step on all the footprints in order. You have done the box step!

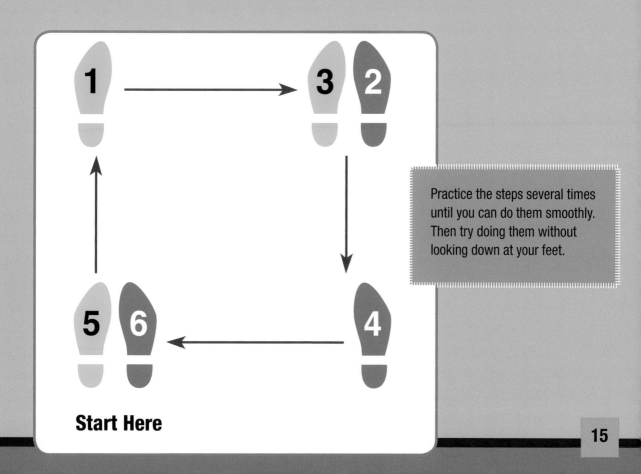

Practice the steps several times until you can do them smoothly. Then try doing them without looking down at your feet.

Start Here

Latin Dances

International Latin dances include the **samba**, the **rumba**, the **cha-cha**, the **paso doble**, and the **jive**. They are usually danced to Latin American music.

Samba

The samba began with African dances. African slaves brought these dances to Brazil. The samba gradually became known in Brazil's cities at the end of the 1800s. It became popular in the United States and Europe in the 1940s. Carmen Miranda, a Brazilian singer, helped to make samba music and dancing popular.

During the samba, dancers' bodies rock back and forth. The dance has quick steps backward and forward. It is often performed to lively Latin music.

Carmen Miranda was a movie star and singer. She was known for her fruit-filled hats.

Carnival in Brazil

Each year, the Brazilian city of Rio de Janeiro holds a celebration called Carnival. More than 70 groups called samba clubs compete during parades. Even small samba clubs may have more than 1,000 members!

Samba dancers wear colorful costumes during Carnival in Brazil.

Rumba

The rumba came from Cuba. Like the samba, it started with African dances. It spread throughout the United States and Europe in the 1930s. Cuban orchestras helped to make the dance popular. In 1935 there was even a movie called *Rumba*.

The rumba has a quick-quick-slow **rhythm**. The dancer bends and straightens his or her knees, one at a time. This makes the dancer's hips sway from side to side.

Cha-cha

The cha-cha is related to a Cuban dance called the **mambo**. The cha-cha's rhythm makes it easy to recognize. You can count the rhythm as slow-slow-quick-quick-slow, or step-step-cha-cha-cha. The dance became popular in the 1950s. In some cha-cha steps, partners do not touch each other. In this way, it is like the dances to rock music that followed in later years.

Paso doble

Paso doble means "double step" in Spanish. This dance from Spain is based on the movements of a bullfight. The man moves like a bullfighter. The woman moves like the bullfighter's cape. She swirls and spins around her partner. The paso doble features dramatic poses and music with a marching beat. It is mostly danced in competitions.

Jive

A fast, bouncy dance called the **jitterbug** became popular in the 1930s. It was danced to a type of jazz music called swing. The jitterbug and other **swing** dances began in the United States. During the jitterbug, a man might swing his dance partner around in the air. The jive is a tamer version of the jitterbug. Men are not allowed to lift their partner during a jive competition.

The Savoy Ballroom was a dance hall in Harlem, a neighborhood in New York City. Many say the jitterbug started there.

PERFORMANCE ACTIVITY

Try the jitterbug!

Face a friend and join hands. One of you can do the steps described below. These steps are shown next to the boy in the picture. The other can do the mirror image. These steps are shown next to the girl in the picture.

Steps to follow:

1. Take a medium-sized step to the left, putting your weight on your left foot. Count "one-two" as you step.

2. Step onto your right foot. Count "three-four."

3. Step behind your right foot with your left toe as you count "five." Put your weight on your left toe, but only for a second—it's quick!

4. Quickly step onto your right foot again as you count "six."

5. Now put on some music and dance! Try dancing to a classic song such as "Hound Dog" by Elvis Presley or a modern song with a fast beat.

The steps might feel awkward at first. As you do them more, they will start to feel natural. Then you can really start dancing!

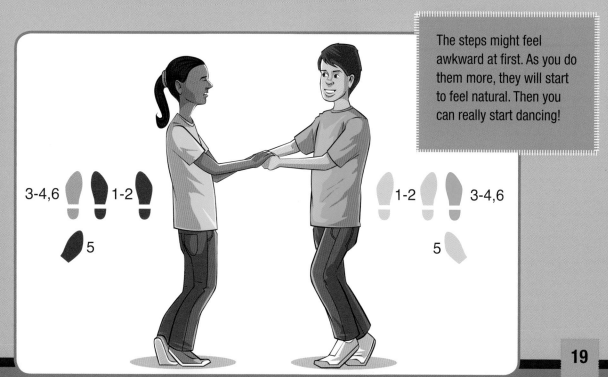

New Directions

Ballroom dances have changed over time. Some partner dances have fallen out of style. New dances have appeared. Television and movies often help new dances to spread.

Come Dancing, a television show in the United Kingdom, began airing in 1949. At first it taught viewers how to do various dances. Later it became a dance competition show. *Come Dancing* ran for more than 40 years.

In the 1950s, a television show called *American Bandstand* began in the United States. It showed a roomful of teenagers doing dances such as the **jitterbug**. The show brought dancing into living rooms across the country.

Many Americans first saw the jitterbug when it was performed on television.

Modern dances

Around 1960 U.S. singer Chubby Checker recorded a song called "The Twist." He did a dance called the **twist** on *American Bandstand*. The twist is a simple dance. You just swivel your hips and feet. It can be done without a partner. You do not need to take lessons. Both the dance and the song became wildly popular.

The **salsa** is a Latin dance related to the **cha-cha** and other Cuban dances. It started in the mid-1960s. It became popular again during the 1990s. Today, salsa clubs can be found around the world.

In the 1970s, clubs and radio stations began to play disco music. A disco dance called the **hustle** swept into nightclubs. A 1977 movie called *Saturday Night Fever* helped to make the hustle popular.

Ice dancing

Ballroom dancing has had an impact on sports. Ice dancing is like ballroom dancing on ice skates. Since they are on skates, dancers can take long, gliding steps. Ice dancing has been an Olympic sport since 1976.

Like ballroom dancers, ice dancers perform **waltzes**, **fox-trots**, and other dances.

Dancing to Win

Many people do ballroom dances for fun. This is called social dancing. There are certain steps that can be done for each dance. But there is no special order in which they must be danced. The leader decides which step to do. He uses his body to tell the follower which step is next.

Other people dance to take part in competitions. In dance competitions, dancers perform routines that they have practiced. Judges watch them and decide which couple wins.

Some dancers compete only in local contests. But some travel all over the world to compete. To compete at the top levels, dancers train for years. They spend a lot of money on lessons and costumes (see box above). They stay in very good physical shape.

Ballroom dance competitions are held all over the world.

Judging the dancers

During a competition, many couples dance at the same time. Judges walk around and give each couple a score. The judges pay attention to many things. Do the dancers have good posture? Are they dancing in time to the music? Does their dancing show the music's emotion? If there is a "traffic jam" on the dance floor, do they avoid running into other couples? Do they look like they are having fun? All the judges' scores are combined to find the winning couple.

Judges watch each couple dance during a competition.

Art or Sport?

The Summer Olympic Games are held every four years. People come from all over the world to compete in different sports. Some people feel there should be ballroom dance competitions in the Olympics, but others disagree.

Dance as art

Some people who do not want ballroom dancing included in the Olympics feel there are enough Olympic sports already. Others do not want it included because they think of dance as an art rather than a sport. Still others object to the way ballroom dancing is judged. Each judge scores dancers slightly differently. Unlike in a race, there is often no clear winner. Furthermore, some dancers feel that the Olympics would take attention away from other ballroom dance contests.

It is easy to tell who wins a footrace. Ballroom dancing is more difficult to judge.

In synchronized swimming, people swim together while music plays. Some people feel that if this sport is in the Olympics, ballroom dancing should be, too.

Dance as sport

On the other hand, there are many reasons to include ballroom dancing in the Olympics. Dancing well takes training and dedication. In this way it is like gymnastics, diving, and other Olympic sports. To compete at the top levels, dancers must be in good shape. Tests show that top dancers doing a short dance need to work as hard as runners in an 800-meter race. Ballroom dancing is an event in which women and men could compete together.

Today, competitive ballroom dancing is called DanceSport. The name was changed to show that this type of dancing is now considered to be a sport. Perhaps one day, ballroom dancers will compete for Olympic gold medals, just as runners and gymnasts do.

Ballroom: Back in Style

In the second half of the 1900s, ballroom dancing became less popular. People wanted to dance without having to learn steps. If you dance to rock music, you can do anything you want. You do not even need a partner.

But ballroom dancing is making a comeback. Television shows such as *Dancing with the Stars* have introduced millions to ballroom dancing (see box at right). *Shall We Dance?* and other movies featuring ballroom dancing have also helped interest to grow.

Now more people are taking ballroom dance lessons. Some elementary schools teach students ballroom dancing. The students sometimes have a chance to compete in dance contests. Studios and ballrooms teach adults how to dance. They also host dance parties where people can practice what they learn.

Ballroom dancing on television

In *Dancing with the Stars*, dance teams compete against one another. Each team is made up of one professional dancer and one famous person who is *not* a dancer. The teams learn routines and then perform them on television. Viewers vote to pick the winner each week.

Many senior centers offer dance lessons for older adults.

Dance competitions

Many people enjoy taking part in dance competitions. Dance groups hold events where people can compete at different levels. Many colleges have ballroom dance teams. They compete against one another, just as other sports teams do.

Ballroom dance challenges both the mind and the body. It mixes elegance with fun. It is a good way to meet people and to get a good workout. It is no wonder that ballroom dancing is popular again.

Wheelchair dancing is popular in many countries. In a style called combi-dance, only one member of a team uses a wheelchair (as shown here). In a style called duo-dance, two wheelchair users dance together.

Timeline

1812	The **Viennese waltz** comes to England.
1907	The **tango** becomes popular in France.
1912	The tango becomes popular in England.
1914	The **fox-trot** begins in New York City.
1927	The **quickstep** begins.
1928	The first "all-talking" feature film, *Lights of New York*, is released.
	Regular television broadcasts begin.
1930s	The **rumba** becomes popular in the United States and Europe.
	The **jitterbug** starts in the United States.
1933	Fred Astaire and Ginger Rogers make their first movie together, *Flying Down to Rio*.

1940s	The **samba** becomes popular.
1940	Carmen Miranda makes her first Hollywood film, *Down Argentine Way*.
1950s	The **cha-cha** becomes popular.
1960	Chubby Checker sings "The Twist" on *American Bandstand*. A dance called the **twist** becomes very popular.
1970s	The **hustle** becomes popular.
1977	The movie *Saturday Night Fever* fuels interest in the hustle and other dances.
2005	*Dancing with the Stars* first appears on television in the United States.

Glossary

bolero slow Latin dance related to the rumba

Boston slow kind of waltz with long, smooth steps

cha-cha dance with a slow-slow-quick-quick-slow rhythm

closed position dance position in which the leader and the follower face each other and hold their bodies close together

composer person who writes music

folk dance dance of a nation's common people

fox-trot gliding dance often done to big-band music

hustle dance popular in the 1970s

International Latin group of dances that includes the cha-cha, rumba, samba, paso doble, and jive

International Standard group of dances that includes the waltz, fox-trot, tango, quickstep, and Viennese waltz

jitterbug dance popular in the 1930s and 1940s in which the man often swings or lifts his partner into the air

jive lively, bouncy dance with kicks and feet flicks

line of dance imaginary counterclockwise circle on the dance floor

mambo Cuban dance popular in the 1950s

minuet French dance that was popular in the 1600s

open position dance position in which the leader and the follower may join hands, but need not face each other

paso doble Spanish dance in which dancers move like a bullfighter and his cape

progressive dance dance in which partners move around the ballroom following the line of dance

quickstep fast, gliding dance with hops and running steps

rhythm pattern of beats in music

rumba dance with side-to-side hip movement

salsa Latin dance popular in clubs

samba dance with small steps and a rocking movement

spot dance dance in which partners stay in the same area of the ballroom

swing group of dances often danced to a certain kind of jazz music

tango dramatic dance combining smooth and quick movements

triple meter rhythm in which the beats in the music come in groups of three

twist dance made popular in the 1960s by U.S. musician Chubby Checker

Viennese waltz fast waltz that has lots of turns

waltz smooth ballroom dance done to music that has beats grouped in threes

Find Out More

Books

Freese, Joan. *Ballroom Dancing* (*Snap*). Mankato, Minn.: Capstone, 2008.

Gillis, Jennifer Blizin. *Ballroom Dancing for Fun!* Minneapolis: Compass Point, 2008.

Hodge, Susie. *Latin and Ballroom* (*Dance*). Chicago: Heinemann Library, 2009.

Websites

USA Dance, Member Organization of the U.S. Olympic Committee
http://usadance.org

America's Ballroom Challenge
www.pbs.org/wgbh/ballroomchallenge

Ballroom Dancers' Federation International
www.bdfi.org

International DanceSport Federation
www.idsf.net

DVD

Mad Hot Ballroom, directed by Marilyn Agrelo (Paramount, 2005).
This documentary film shows children in New York City preparing for a ballroom dance competition.

Index

African dances 16, 17
allemande 10
American Bandstand 20, 21
American Rhythm dances 6
American Smooth dances 6
Argentina 11, 14
Astaire, Fred 13

ballroom dancing
  American style 6
  earliest ballroom dances
    10–11
  International Latin dances
    6, 7, 8, 16–18
  International Standard
    dances 6, 7, 8, 12–14
  International style 6
bolero 6
Boston (slow waltz) 13
box step 15
Brazil 11, 16, 17

Carnival 17
cha-cha 6, 8, 16, 17, 21
Charleston 14
Checker, Chubby 21
closed position 7, 12
Come Dancing 20
communication 4
competitions 5, 22–23, 26, 27
  DanceSport 25
  judging 23, 24
  Olympic Games 21, 24–25
costumes 22
Cuban dances 17, 21

DanceSport 25
Dancing with the Stars 26
disco dances 21
dramatic poses 14, 18

earliest ballroom dances
  10–11
East Coast swing 6

folk dances 11
fox-trot 6, 12, 14, 21

hustle 21

ice dancing 21
International Latin dances
  6, 7, 8, 16–18
International Standard dances
  6, 7, 8, 12–14

jitterbug 18, 19, 20
jive 6, 7, 8, 16, 18

Lanner, Josef 12
leaders and followers 4
lessons 26
line of dance 8

mambo 6, 17
minuet 10
Miranda, Carmen 16

Olympic Games 21, 24–25
open position 6

paso doble 6, 8, 16, 18
pavane 10
posture 23
progressive dances 8

quickstep 6, 12, 14

rhythms 5, 9, 17
rock music 26
Rogers, Ginger 13
rumba 6, 8, 15, 16, 17

salsa 21
samba 6, 7, 8, 11, 16–17
Saturday Night Fever 21
social dancing 22
Spain 18
spot dances 8
Strauss, Johann 12
swing 6, 18
synchronized swimming 25

tango 6, 11, 12, 14
tap dance 13
triple meter 9, 12, 13
twist 21

Vienna Opera Ball 12
Viennese waltz 6, 11, 12, 13

waltz 4, 6, 9, 11, 12, 13,
  15, 21
  Boston (slow waltz) 13
  Viennese waltz 6, 11, 12, 13
wheelchair dancing 27
  combi-dance 27
  duo-dance 27

7/2/15
J.H.